T5-CQE-054

For

WHEN YOU WISH
UPON A STAR

Compiled by Liesl Vazquez

Illustrated by Jenny Faw

Peter Pauper Press, Inc.
White Plains, New York

For my mother and father

Copyright © 1995
Peter Pauper Press, Inc.
202 Mamaroneck Avenue
White Plains, NY 10601
All rights reserved
ISBN 0-88088-792-3
Printed in China
7 6 5 4 3 2 1

WHEN YOU WISH
UPON A STAR

Far away there in the sunshine are my highest aspirations. I may not reach them, but I can look up and see their beauty, believe in them, and try to follow where they lead.

Louisa May Alcott

S hoot for the moon. Even
if you miss it you will
land among the stars.

Les Brown

Dreams, like kind words, linger warmly about us and fill us with delight and inspiration.

Lori Monroe

We are such stuff
As dreams are made
on, and our little life
Is rounded with a sleep.
William Shakespeare

L ook behind the clouds.
You will always find the
stars.

Evelyn Loeb

My dreams know no boundaries. They fly freely on wings of light to the moon, the stars, and beyond.

Angela Freer

Stars are diamonds in the sky and wishes make them sparkle.

Evelyn Loeb

Meet me in Dreamland,
sweet dreamy
Dreamland,
There let my dreams come
true.

Beth Slater Whitson

B e thankful in the morning, complacent in the daytime, wistful as the sun sets. But let your dreams take flight at the twinkling of the first star.

Jules Beame

What is love? . . . It is the morning and the evening star.

Sinclair Lewis

Wishes are the touch-
stones of our dreams.

Jesse Rogers

I do not know whether I was then a man dreaming I was a butterfly, or whether I am now a butterfly dreaming I am a man.

Chuang Tse

Don't be afraid of the space between your dreams and reality. If you can dream it, you can make it so.

Belva Davis

If you have built castles in the air, your work need not be lost; that is where they should be. Now put the foundations under them.

Henry David Thoreau

I magination is the highest
kite one can fly.

Lauren Bacall

All that we see or
       seem
Is but a dream within a
   dream.

Edgar Allan Poe

Dreams are necessary to
life.

Anaïs Nin

H itch your wagon to a
star.

Ralph Waldo Emerson

I arise from dreams of thee
In the first sweet sleep of
  night.
When the winds are breath-
  ing low,
And the stars are shining
  bright.

Percy Bysshe Shelley,
The Indian Serenade

In your dreams, search for the pot of gold at the end of the rainbow. In your life, search for the rainbow.

Hope McKnight

My father gathers wool
My mother shuttles
    yarn
But I am a weaver of
dreams.

Maggie Miller

Oh, Jerry, don't let's ask for the moon: we have the stars.

Spoken by Bette Davis, in movie Now Voyager

A #2 pencil and a dream can take you anywhere.

Joyce A. Myers

S addle your dreams afore
you ride 'em.

Mary Webb

I have spread my dreams
under your feet.
Tread softly because you
tread on my dreams.

W. B. Yeats

There is no medicine like hope, no incentive so great, and no tonic so powerful as expectation of something tomorrow.

O. S. Marden

Ye stars, that are the poet-
ry of heaven!

Lord Byron

The wonder is what you can make a paradise out of.

Eva Hoffman

The dream, alone, is of interest. What is life, without a dream?

Edmond Rostand,
La Princesse Lointaine

It isn't a calamity to die
with dreams unfulfilled,
but it is a calamity not to
dream.

Benjamin Mays

I dreamed that, as I wandered by the way,
   Bare Winter suddenly
   was changed to
   Spring,
And gentle odours led my
steps astray,
   Mixed with a sound of
   water's murmuring

Along a shelving bank of
turf, which lay
   Under a copse,
   and hardly dared to
   fling
Its green arms round the
bosom of the stream,
   But kissed it and then fled,
   as thou mightst in dream.
        Percy Bysshe Shelley,
        The Question

E very wish is like a
prayer with God.
Elizabeth Barrett Browning

When I dream
I am always ageless.
Elizabeth Coatsworth

There was a time when
meadow, grove, and
stream,
The earth, and every common sight,
To me did seem
Apparelled in celestial
light,
The glory and the freshness
of a dream.

William Wordsworth

No one can have all he wants, but a man can refrain from wanting what he has not, and cheerfully make the best of a bird in the hand.

Seneca

The evening star, love's harbinger, appeared.

Milton

Silent, one by one, in the infinite meadows of heaven, blossomed the lovely stars, the forget-me-nots of angels.

Longfellow

There are two tragedies in life. One is to lose your heart's desire. The other is to gain it.

George Bernard Shaw

Wishes and dreams are born in the comforting realities of everyday pleasures.

Julie Turner

Dreams come true in every bouquet of flowers handed to a loved one.

Alison Leigh

D reaming permits each
and every one of us to
be quietly and safely insane
every night of our lives.
William Dement

D o not wish to be any-
thing but what you are,
and try to be that perfectly.

St. Francis de Sales

The future belongs to
those who believe in the
beauty of their dreams.

Eleanor Roosevelt

The smallest of wishes begins in the imagination but unfolds among galaxies of stars and realized dreams.

Kayla Randall

Every time a wish comes true, the dim light of a faraway star transforms into a new, brilliant radiance.

Nicole Weisman

The dreams and wishes
two people share allow
love to shine like the bright-
est star on a clear spring
night.

Marie Sanders

A flicker of starlight, like a rainbow or a snowflake, is nature's way of granting wishes.

Liesl Vazquez

I f not for our dreams, to
what would we aspire?

L. M. Santiago

It is sometimes necessary to confuse fantasy for reality and dreaming for waking. Doing so enables us to experience wish fulfillment, and then to strive for it wholeheartedly.

Liesl Vazquez

Never give up on your
childhood dreams;
adulthood affords the
opportunity to realize them.

Nancy Masco

Open your mind, as well as your heart, to the magical warmth of wishes and dreams.

Linda St. James

Often, the sweetest delight comes from the fulfillment of a forgotten dream.

Vanessa Parede

L earn to listen to the orchestra of stars: the peal of wishes fulfilled and the chime of dreams come true ring through the skies with glory.

Margaret Carpio

Star light—opening our hearts
Star bright—expanding our sight
May we have the wish we wish tonight.

Nicole Beale

Wishes are splendid
flowers that decorate
my mind and enrich my
soul with color and fra-
grance.

Alisa Dennison

The pleasure of the true dreamer does not lie in the substance of the dream, but in this: that there things happen without any interference from his side, and altogether outside his control.

Isak Dinesen

When you reach for the stars, you may not quite get one, but you won't come up with a handful of mud either.

Leo Burnett

If a man wants his dreams to come true, he must wake up.

Anonymous

In the depths of night,
under the deepest sky,
often come thoughts that
sparkle like the stars above.
Nicole Beale

I had a wonderful dream last night—don't miss it.

Groucho Marx

I like the dreams of the
future better than the his-
tory of the past.

Thomas Jefferson

It is difficult to say what is impossible, for the dream of yesterday is the hope of today and the reality of tomorrow.

Robert H. Goddard